CAMDEN COUNTY LIBRARY
203 LAUREL ROAD
VOORHEES, NJ 08043
CCLS - Rutgers

0500000538984 1

J953.8    Anderson, Abby.
And
         Saudi Arabia

W9-BBA-354

# SAUDI ARABIA

COUNTRY EXPLORERS

Abby Anderson

Lerner Publications Company • Minneapolis

Copyright © 2009 by Lerner Publishing Group, Inc.

All rights reserved. International copyright secured. No part of this book may be reproduced, stored in a retrieval system, or transmitted in any form or by any means—electronic, mechanical, photocopying, recording, or otherwise—without the prior written permission of Lerner Publishing Group, Inc., except for the inclusion of brief quotations in an acknowledged review.

Lerner Publications Company
A division of Lerner Publishing Group, Inc.
241 First Avenue North
Minneapolis, MN 55401 U.S.A.

Website address: www.lernerbooks.com

Library of Congress Cataloging-in-Publication Data

Anderson, Abby.
    Saudi Arabia / by Abby Anderson.
        p.   cm. — (Country explorers)
    Includes index.
    ISBN 978-1-58013-595-5 (lib. bdg. : alk. paper)
    1. Saudi Arabia—Juvenile literature.  I. Title.
DS204.25.A532  2009
953.8—dc22                          2008008723

Manufactured in the United States of America
1 2 3 4 5 6 – PA – 14 13 12 11 10 09

# Table of Contents

## Welcome!

We're visiting Saudi Arabia! This country is in the Middle East. The Middle East is the part of Asia that meets Africa and Europe.

The Red Sea lies west of Saudi Arabia. To the north are Jordan and Iraq. Kuwait sits to the east. So do the Persian Gulf, Qatar, and the United Arab Emirates. Oman and Yemen are to the south.

Saudi Arabia is on the Arabian Peninsula. A peninsula is a piece of land with water on three sides. The Red Sea (*right*) laps the Arabian Peninsula.

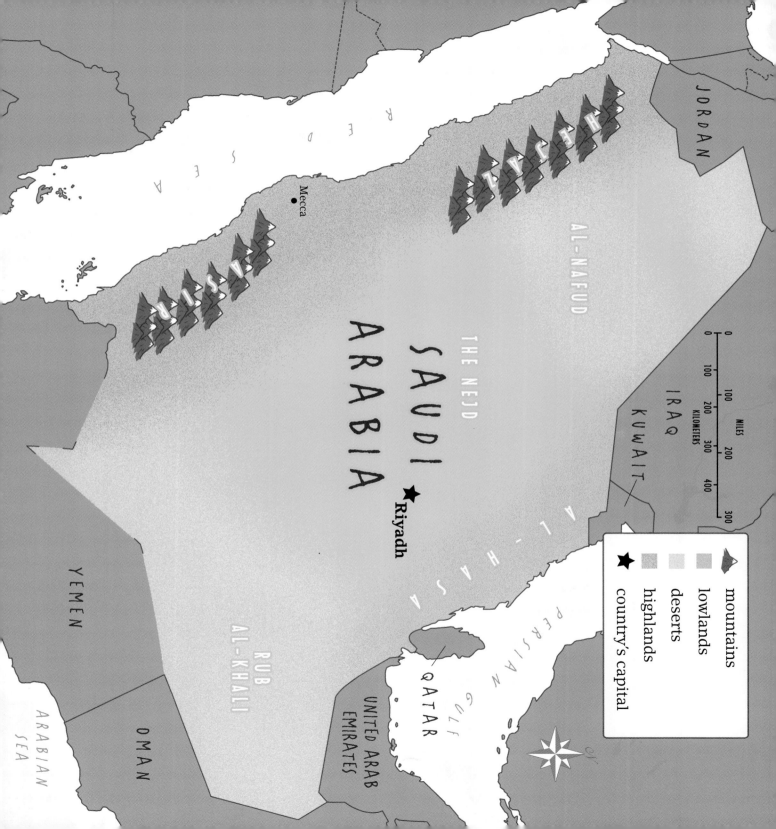

JORDAN

RED SEA

Mecca

AL-NAFUD

HIJAZ

SAUDI
ARABIA

THE NEJD

ASIR

Riyadh

IRAQ

KUWAIT

AL-HASA

YEMEN

RUB
AL-KHALI

OMAN

UNITED ARAB
EMIRATES

QATAR

PERSIAN GULF

ARABIAN
SEA

MILES
0
100
200
300

KILOMETERS
0
100
200
300
400

★  mountains
   lowlands
   deserts
   highlands
★  country's capital

## Across the Country

Much of Saudi Arabia is desert—but not all of it. The Hejaz region runs along the Red Sea's coast. Beaches and cliffs rise to hills and mountains.

The Asir region is south of Hejaz. Mountains and farmland lie there.

Farm fields cover the land in the Asir region.

Large, rocky plateaus stretch to the east. This area is called the Nejd. Oases dot the Nejd. Lush oases are moist places in a desert.

North of the Nejd is al-Nafud Desert. This desert has reddish sand dunes.

Crops grow at this oasis in the Nejd.

## Map Whiz Quiz

Check out the map on page 5. A map is a drawing or chart of a place.

Trace the map onto a sheet of paper. See if you can find the Red Sea. Color it red, and mark it with a W for west. Now see if you can find the Persian Gulf. Color it blue, and mark it with an E for East.

## Deserts and Oil

A desert called Rub al-Khali lies in the southeast. It's the biggest sandy desert in the world! It's also the hottest and driest place on Earth. Temperatures can reach 120°F (49°C).

The Rub al-Khali Desert gets extremely hot in summer months. This desert is almost as big as Texas!

Sand and gravel plains border the Persian Gulf. This dry land is called al-Hasa. Oil lies beneath al-Hasa. People drill wells to bring the oil to the surface.

People send oil from al-Hasa to this factory at the edge of the desert. People use the oil to make gasoline.

## Family Life

Saudi families are very close. Kids often live near grandparents, aunts, uncles, and cousins. The family might get together once a week.

A family enjoys a day at the beach in Saudi Arabia.

## Family Words

Saudi Arabian families speak Arabic. Here are the Arabic names for family members.

| | | |
|---|---|---|
| grandfather | jeddee | (ZHED-ee) |
| grandmother | jeddatee | (ZHED-ah-tee) |
| father | eb | (EHB) |
| mother | omun | (OH-moon) |
| uncle | omi | (AAHM-ee) |
| aunt | omti | (AAHM-tee) |
| brother | okh | (OAK) |
| sister | okht | (OH-kit) |
| son | wuld | (WILD) |
| daughter | bent | (BINT) |

Most Saudi Arabian women raise children and run the house. Men usually go to work and do the shopping. In modern times, some women may also have careers. But most do not. Women typically stay close to home.

11

Arab men ride camels in a parade through the city. Arabs are proud of their history and culture.

## The Saudis

More than 20 million people live in Saudi Arabia. Most Saudis belong to an ethnic group called the Arabs.

Arabs are linked by their language and their history. They have lived in the area for thousands of years.

This boy lives in a village that is hundreds of years old.

## Desert Nomads

Some Saudi Arabian Arabs are nomads. Nomads are people who move from place to place.

Saudi nomads herd goats and sheep. They camp in tents made from goat or camel hair.

Saudi nomads camp with their camel herds in the desert.

Most modern-day nomads stay near hospitals and schools. That way, kids can go to classes and sick people can get treatment.

Visitors to a Saudi nomad camp share a meal.

## Nomadic Traditions

Many Saudis lived as nomads in the past. Saudi culture comes from nomadic traditions. One of these traditions is generosity to guests. No one can live alone in the desert, so nomads treat their guests like family.

Jidda is a large city in Saudia Arabia.

## City Saudis

Most Saudi Arabians live in cities. Modern cities have schools, hospitals, roads, and malls. Gardens with fountains and pools of water dot the cities.

City dwellers live in houses or apartments with two living rooms. One is for men, and the other is for women.

Saudi men drink coffee in a living room set aside for them.

## Religion

Islam is the religion of Saudi Arabia. All Saudi Arabians follow Islam. People who follow Islam are called Muslims.

Muslims visit an Islamic place of worship.

Muslims believe in one God, called Allah. They believe a prophet named Muhammad received Allah's messages. The messages became the Quran (the Islamic holy book). Kids celebrate the first time they read the Quran.

A schoolgirl reads from the Quran.

## A Sacred Time

Ramadan is a sacred time for Muslims. Ramadan is the Islamic holy month. Muslims fast from dawn to sunset during Ramadan. That means they do not eat or drink. After dark, they pray at a mosque (an Islamic place of worship). Then they eat a big meal.

## Times to Pray

Muslims pray at dawn, noon, midafternoon, sunset, and nightfall. Business stops at prayer time.

Children stop for midafternoon prayer at school.

Before praying, Muslims wash themselves. They face Mecca. That's a city in western Saudi Arabia. Muhammad was born in Mecca. It's the holiest city of Islam.

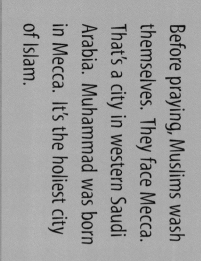

Crowds of people pray at a mosque in Mecca. All Muslims try to visit Mecca at least once.

## Cover Up!

Many Saudis wear traditional clothing. Men wear a long shirt called a *thobe*. It goes all the way to the ground. They may also cover their heads with a square of cotton cloth. A black cord holds the cloth in place.

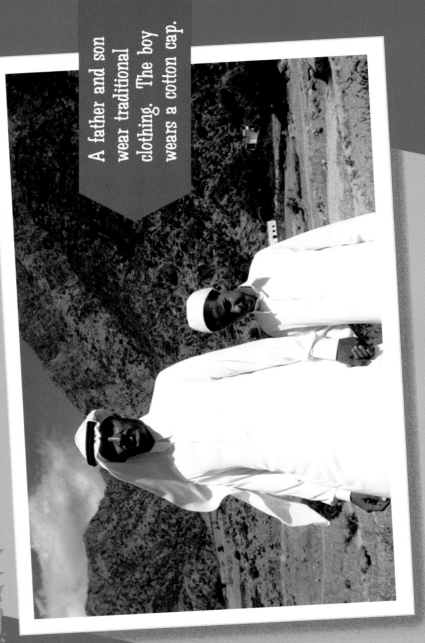

A father and son wear traditional clothing. The boy wears a cotton cap.

Women may wear jeans and casual tops at home. But in public, they wear a robe called an abaya. The abaya goes over a woman's clothes. It covers her whole body.

Saudi women wear abayas while shopping. The abayas are a sign of their modesty.

## Modesty

Modesty is important to Saudi Arabians. It is part of their religious faith. Saudi Arabians take great care to dress modestly in public. Their style of dress reflects their Islamic values.

## Kid Life

A family's love surrounds a Saudi child. Families help kids decide what to study at school, what kind of job to have, and whom to marry.

A Saudi family enjoys a ride at a fair.

Kids respect their older relatives. Children listen to older people and follow their advice.

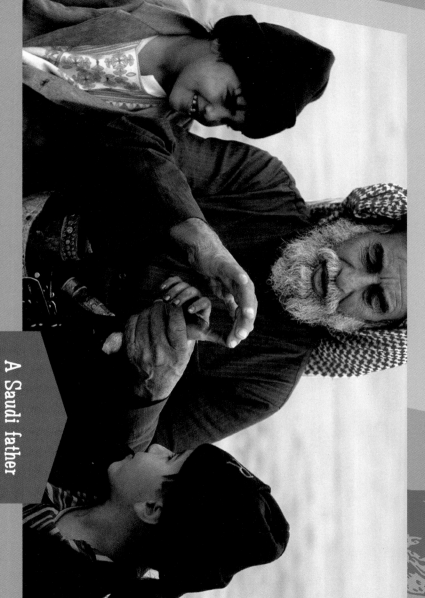

A Saudi father plays with his daughters. They live in a nomad camp.

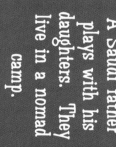

## Souk Shopping

A souk, or marketplace, is an exciting spot to visit. The air smells of coffee and rich spices. Gold jewelry flashes in the sun.

Many different items are for sale at a souk. You might find clothing, tasty foods, or pretty rugs.

Men sell fruit, spices, and grain at a souk in Saudi Arabia.

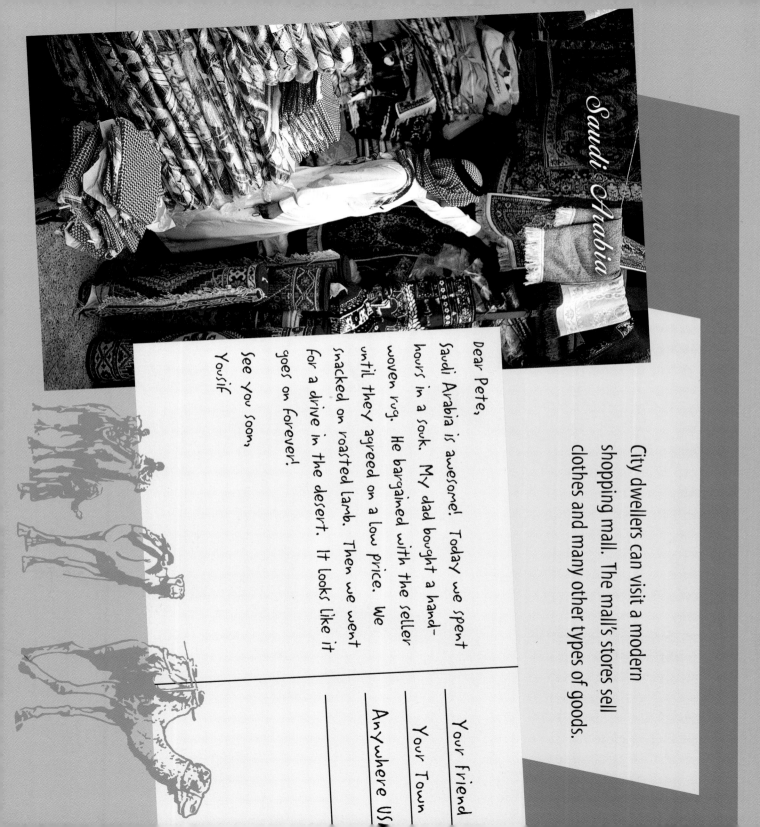

*Saudi Arabia*

City dwellers can visit a modern shopping mall. The mall's stores sell clothes and many other types of goods.

Dear Pete,

Saudi Arabia is awesome! Today we spent hours in a souk. My dad bought a hand-woven rug. He bargained with the seller until they agreed on a low price. We snacked on roasted lamb. Then we went for a drive in the desert. It looks like it goes on forever!

See you soon,
Yousif

Your friend
Your Town
Anywhere US

## Arabic ABCs

Arabic is the language of Saudi Arabia. The Arabic alphabet doesn't look like the alphabet that English speakers know.

These books and pages show Arabic writing.

People write Arabic from right to left. Readers turn book pages from left to right. That's opposite from the way people read books written in English. But to Saudi Arabians, English-language books look backward!

An artist uses a cut reed to write in Arabic. Most Saudis use pens or pencils to write.

## Poems and Stories

Saudis love poetry! They chant it, write it, and read it.

A Saudi mother reads old stories to her daughter.

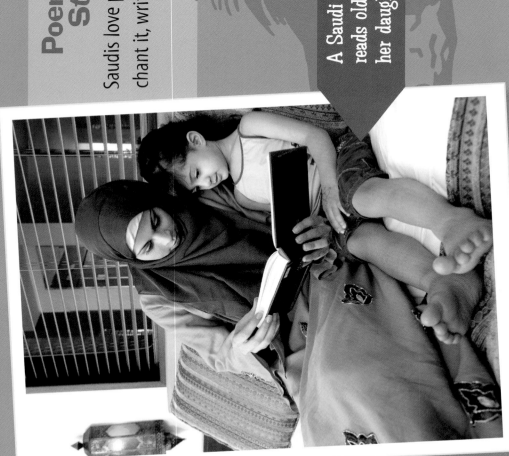

Many Saudis enjoy poems about brave people and daring deeds. Some Saudis enjoy folktales about animals. Stories of magic and wild adventures are popular too.

Saudi men clap along with folk musicians.

## Time for School

Saudi boys and girls don't go to school together. Instead, they study in separate buildings.

Boys work on their homework at a Saudi school.

Kids might learn math, Arabic, history, and science. Some students go on to earn college degrees.

College students study in the school library.

## Big Lunch!

Lunch is the biggest meal of the day in Saudi Arabia. Saudis might eat lettuce, cucumbers, tomatoes, rice, and lamb stew.

Mint and lemon season many dishes. A flat bread called pita is served at every meal.

Men use pieces of pita bread to scoop food out of large pots at a feast.

After lunch, many people rest for a few hours. It's too hot to do much else this time of day! Kids who don't want to nap may read or do their homework.

A man pours tea for a guest. In some parts of Saudi Arabia, people prefer tea to coffee.

## Coffee Break

Serving tiny cups of coffee is a Saudi tradition. The host serves the oldest or most important person first. Saudis consider it polite to drink two cups but not three! To refuse the third serving, a Saudi waggles the cup back and forth.

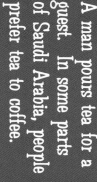

## Carry Your Art

It is hard to find a place for fancy art in a tent—so nomadic Saudis created beautiful everyday objects. These objects included carpets and fancy saddles. Saudis treasure these objects in modern times too.

This carpet decorates the floor of a mosque in Mecca.

A Saudi girl wears jewelry trimmed with bells and colorful tassels.

Many Saudis admire beautiful jewelry. Some Saudis wear five bracelets or rings. Five is considered a lucky number. Children like to wear bell-trimmed anklets and bracelets.

## Sword Dance

Saudi Arabia has a national dance. The dance is called the *ardha*. It's performed with swords.

Saudi men perform the ardha.

38

The ardha is very exciting to watch. Men stand shoulder to shoulder in rows. They all face in the same direction.

In the center of the group, a poet sings. Drummers beat a rhythm. The men step and sway. They wave their swords in the air. The dance can be done with just a few people or with hundreds.

Drummers play for dancers performing the ardha.

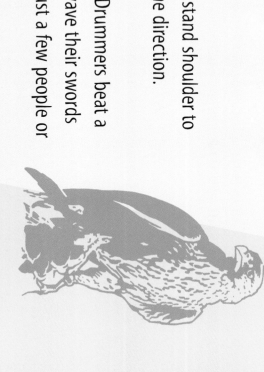

## Celebrate!

A three-day festival marks the end of Ramadan. Families go to mosques. Then they go home to exchange gifts and eat a feast. Many people wear new clothes. They also give gifts to the poor.

Boys dance and play drums to mark the end of Ramadan.

Another fun festival takes place in the spring. It's the Jenadriyah Heritage and Cultural Festival. Saudis celebrate their culture on this day.

Poets recite famous verses. People display many crafts. Dancers perform the ardha.

This boy has decorated his camel. A camel race kicks off the Jenadriyah Heritage and Cultural Festival.

This young man is training his falcon to hunt.

## Fun in Saudi Arabia

Falconry is a traditional Saudi Arabian pastime. This sport involves training falcons to hunt other birds. Saudi falcon trainers treat their falcons with great care.

Many Saudi families enjoy camping in the desert. They pack a picnic lunch to eat.

Campers nap in the hot afternoons. They stay awake at night, when it is cool.

43

Children play soccer on a desert field. Soccer is the most popular team sport in Saudia Arabia.

## THE FLAG OF SAUDI ARABIA

Saudi Arabia's flag is green and white. Green is an important color in Saudi Arabia. It is the color of Islam. It is also thought to be Muhammad's favorite color. Arabic words are in the center of the green flag. The words say, "There is no God but Allah, and Muhammad is his prophet." Below the words lies a sword. The sword shows that Saudis will fight to spread the Islamic faith.

# FAST FACTS

FULL COUNTRY NAME: Kingdom of Saudi Arabia

AREA: 865,000 square miles (2,240,350 square kilometers), or about the same size as the United States east of the Mississippi

MAIN LANDFORMS: the regions Hejaz, Asir, and the Nejd; the deserts al-Nafud and Rub al-Khali; the coastal plain al-Hasa

MAJOR RIVERS: none

ANIMALS AND THEIR HABITATS: dromedary camels (desert), ibex (mountains), baboons (highlands), songbirds called bulbuls (oases)

CAPITAL CITY: Riyadh

OFFICIAL LANGUAGE: Arabic

POPULATION: about 28,161,417

# GLOSSARY

**culture:** the way of life, ideas, and customs of a particular group of people

**desert:** a dry, sandy region

**ethnic group:** a large community of people that shares the same language, religion, and history

**Islam:** a religion that began in Saudi Arabia. Followers of Islam worship Allah.

**map:** a drawing or chart of all or part of Earth or the sky

**Middle East:** the part of Asia that meets Africa and Europe. The Middle East includes the countries extending from Libya in the west to Afghanistan in the east.

**mosque:** an Islamic place of worship

**mountain:** a part of Earth's surface that rises high into the sky

**Muslim:** a follower of Islam

**nomad:** a person who moves from place to place

**oasis:** a moist place in a desert

**plain:** a large, flat area of land

**plateau:** a large area of high, level land

**Quran:** the Islamic holy book

**tradition:** a custom, belief, or practice that people in a particular culture pass on to one another

# TO LEARN MORE

## BOOKS

Douglass, Susan L. *Ramadan*. Minneapolis: Millbrook Press, 2004. Learn more about Ramadan, a holy month for Saudi Arabians and Muslims around the world.

Senker, Cath. *Costume around the World: Saudi Arabia*. New York: Chelsea Clubhouse, 2008. Text and photos explore the clothing people wear in Saudi Arabia.

Temple, Bob. *Welcome to Saudi Arabia*. Mankato, MN: Child's World, 2008. This interesting title features information on Saudi Arabia's geography, people, history, and culture.

Walsh, Kieran. *Saudi Arabia*. Vero Beach, FL: Rourke Publishing, 2004. Learn more about Saudi Arabia in this book, which covers subjects such as school and sports, food and holidays, everyday life, and the country's future.

## WEBSITES

### Enchanted Learning

http://www.enchantedlearning.com/geography

Visit this site to find a Saudi Arabian map and flag that you can color.

### The World Factbook: Saudi Arabia

https://www.cia.gov/library/publications/the-world-factbook/geos/sa.html

This site includes a map of Saudi Arabia as well as in-depth facts that you can use to write reports.

## INDEX

The images in this book are used with the permission of: © arabianEye/arabianEye/Kami, pp. 4, 39; © Helene Rogers/Art Directors & TRIP, p. 6; © Jeremy Horner/drr.net, pp. 7, 42; © arabianEye/Tor Eigeland, p. 8; © Art Directors & TRIP, pp. 9, 26, 31, 32, 35, 37; © AFP/Getty Images, pp. 10, 12; © Wolfgang Kaehler/drr.net, pp. 13, 22; © Thomas J. Abercrombie/Getty Images, p. 14; © Robert Harding/drr.net, p. 15; © John Ellard/Art Directors & TRIP, p. 16; © Robin Laurance/Photolibrary, pp. 17, 20; © Martin Gray/National Geographic/Getty Images, p. 18; © Don Smeltzer/Alamy, p. 19; © GAD/Taxi/Getty Images, p. 21; © Hassan Ammar/AFP/Getty Images, p. 23; © Tom Stoddart/Reportage/Getty Images, p. 24; © Reza/National Geographic/Getty Images, p. 25; © Julian Nieman/Getty Images, p. 27; © arabianEye/arabianEye/JD Dallet, pp. 28, 29; © arabianEye, pp. 30, 33; © Robert Harding Picture Library Ltd/Alamy, p. 34; © Athar Akram/Art Directors & TRIP, p. 36; © Reza/Getty Images, p. 38; ©STR/AFP/Getty Images, p. 40; © FAHAD SHADEED/Getty Images, p. 41; © Julian Nieman/Alamy, p. 41; Illustrations © Bill Hauser/Independent Picture Service.

Front cover: © Reza/National Geographic/Getty Images.

**48**